W D

The Ultimate Guide to Raised Bed Gardening for Beginners

BY LINDSEY PYLARINOS

How to Grow Flowers and Vegetables in Raised Beds for a Successful Garden

2nd Edition

Table Of Contents

Introduction

I want to thank you and congratulate you for purchasing the book, "The Ultimate Guide to Raised Bed Gardening for Beginners: How to Grow Flowers and Vegetables in Raised Beds for A Successful Garden.

In this book, you will find a step by step guide on how you can get started with your own raised bed garden. From building the bed itself, which plants work great for this type of garden and to how to properly tend for it, the information is all in here.

If you're a beginner when it comes to raised bed gardening, you might find yourself continuously going through trial and error. This takes up a lot of time as well as money. Why suffer through that when you can get started with the process the right way? After all, when it comes to gardening, efficiency and timing are important. You wouldn't want to miss out on an abundant yield come spring time, would you?

Let this book take you through the process itself as well as provide you with solutions to the most common problems that gardeners often encounter. No need to feel lost again for all the knowledge you need to get started has been compacted into one single book. All that's left to do is get out there and apply all that you'll learn from it.

Thanks again for purchasing this book, I hope you enjoy it!

Chapter 1: An Overview

If you're looking for something space efficient but can produce high yields, raised bed gardening would be the best option for you to try. Besides being efficient when it comes to space, it also solves a number of other issues such as dealing with difficult soil as well as your garden's accessibility.

But what is it exactly?

Raised bed gardens are basically made up of mounded soil that's surrounded by a frame to make sure it doesn't fall apart. They are usually at least 3 to 4 inches above the ground itself and each "bed" is typically separated by a pathway. Plants would cover the entire surface of these beds and the paths would provide the gardener with ample space to work in, making sure that they don't end up stepping on the soil in the process. A raised bed can be 3 to 5 feet across and the length can vary depending on the need. You'll be able to grow a wide variety of crops vegetables on it as well as herbs. Perennial and annual flowers also thrive in this type of gardening along with roses, shrubs and even berry bushes.

What makes it more efficient?

The thing with raised beds is that it actually provides the best conditions for crop growth. Because the soil in the bed itself tends to be loose, deep and fertile, it results in more efficient yields regardless of what you plant. Of course, there are other factors to consider but for the most part, and if you do the actual planting right, you'll get good results from it.

Raised bed gardens improve a lot of things when compared to more traditional planting styles. It can create a better environment for soil drainage and aeration which allows for the plant roots to penetrate strongly and readily. If weeds happen to grow on it, they're much easier to get rid of. And because of the paths that these beds form, the soil never gets compacted from having been repeatedly stepped on by the gardener.

You must also consider the fact that any improvement you add to the soil remains where it should and won't end up getting wasted on the pathways instead. Typically, these are simply covered with some mulch or planted on with a low growing over-crop. Raised beds are also efficient for another reason, and that's with both time and money. You save on both because there's very little that needs to be done. Because they are compact, your energy wouldn't be spread all over the place and into areas where it would simply go to waste. Each time you garden, you only have to work on each bed and weeds are rare occurrences, given that the crops grow close to each other.

Lastly, if you have limited mobility, this is also a great option for you to consider. Having a wide sill on your framed raised bed provides a great spot to sit on while you tend on your crops. A higher frame would put the crops within the reach of a gardener who makes use of a wheelchair. These beds can be adjusted to fit the need of the person who will be tending to it so even with limited movement, they'll still be able to enjoy this hobby.

What do I need to consider before I start making my first raised bed garden?

While raised bed gardening clearly offers a lot of benefits, it also requires a significant amount of planning. For one, you can expect to shell out quite a bit of money at the beginning. Unless you already have a decent array of shovels and other similar gardening tools, you may have to hit the nearby gardening supplies store to acquire such. Having to rearrange the current soil composition in your backyard may also make the purchase of additional fertilizer necessary.

Furthermore, given that raised beds are equipped with a more efficient water drainage feature, you can also expect your water bills to increase significantly (Raised beds will need to be watered more often than regular flower or vegetable plots.). In some cases, you might also need to purchase and install an irrigation system specifically for the purpose of keeping the soil in a raised bed moist. Evidently, doing so will not come cheap.

Lastly, you need to take special care in planning the dimensions of your flower or vegetable bed. It's important to keep in mind just how many of a certain flower or vegetable you would like to plant in a single bed so you can ensure that they all have enough room to grow (While raised beds do offer the advantage of space efficiency, overcrowding isn't ideal for any sort of plant either.). Also, you shouldn't forget to plan the width of your flower or vegetable bed in such a way that you wouldn't have much difficulty reaching its middle portion, be it to pluck a flower, pick out a vegetable, or simply to water any seedlings growing in the said location. Making a flower or vegetable bed too wide in such a way that you would need to contort your body in different positions just to reach a specific portion would defeat the ergonomic advantages offered by the raised bed method.

Are there any alternatives or similar methods?

Should your raised bed gardening seem a little too free-form for your taste, there are suitable alternatives. Container gardening, for instance, is especially ideal for those who want to make efficient use of their limited gardening space but are constrained by the less-than-desirable quality of their soil. As with raised bed gardening, container gardening elevates the flower or vegetable plot significantly above the usual ground level. The key difference, as its name suggests, is that container gardening makes use of certain holders (wooden frames are especially popular) to do so, as opposed to simply building up the soil into a lofty shape. Gardening containers or frames are usually built with latticed bottoms to allow the water to drain out, and are also designed to enable a raised flower or vegetable bed to hold its shape better in the face of disturbances caused by the elements (such as inclement weather), wayward pets, or by people who might happen to fall or stumble upon them. Container gardening can also help you segregate the more fertile portions of your soil from all the rest, and can also make a raised bed garden look more organized and aesthetically appealing.

Chapter 2: Building The Raised Beds

Ready to get started? Well, the first thing that needs to be done is building the actual bed itself. The most common way of doing so would be making use of the **double-dig**. This process would involve the removal of the topsoil layer then loosening the subsoil before putting the first layer back on top. You would need to mix in a lot of organic matter during this stage, to make sure that the soil is health and well-fertilized. While it can be time-consuming, using the double-dig method has plenty of benefits.

Is there an easier way?

Of course! One of the quickest ways of accomplishing this task is simply scattering a lot of organic matter onto your garden soil. Compost and well-rotted manure as well as bits of shredded leaves would be the most affordable by-products that you can use for this purpose. Now, while the organic content of your soil keeps on increasing, begin to mound up your planting beds. Shape your soil in an unframed bed, make sure that it is flat at the top and has sloping sides. The slope of the sides would help you conserve water.

Eventually, this soil would spread out thus the need for you to hill it up using a hoe ever so often. The frame around its edges would prevent the soil from completely washing away and also allows for you to add even greater depth to it. The most common materials used for framing would include bricks, wood and even unused cement blocks. If you're going for wood, make sure that you choose something that's rot-resistant such as locust, cypress or cedar. Chemically treated wood is an absolute no-no in this case. You would want to keep everything as natural as possible.

This is where you also consider certain improvements to the height of the bed itself if the gardener who would be working on it has certain movement limitations.

What if you're dealing with difficult soil?

Difficult soil would include one that's very alkaline, is made up of heavy clay or is full of rocks. To deal with this, you would want to mix it with some trucked-in topsoil as well as number of mineral additions along with your usual organic matter. From there, you can build up the gardening beds without having to make use of the "difficult" or native soil.

Lasagna Gardening:

If you live in an area where the soil is in great condition for gardening then this is a no-till option that you should give a try. It is a process that's quite similar to sheet composting and would allow you to build your raised beds without having to strip the site of weeds or grass. If you have a previous vegetable garden already in existence and have no time to remove it by bit, then this is something that you should also consider.

Starting on a new site? The first thing you need to do is cut the grass as short as you possibly can. If you have weeds, scalp it at ground level. Next, cover the area for your bed with about 6 sheets of newspaper (thicker would work too and the max is 10 sheets) in order to smother the vegetation that already exists there. If there are perennial weeds on the area, using something thicker such as cardboard or flattened boxes would do the trick. To weigh this down, you can either wet them or pile on mulch on top of the whole area. If you're working with both newspaper and cardboard, make sure that you have their edges overlapping.

Once you're done with that, start layering your organic matter on the area. Combine the materials in the same way you would a compost pole. Mix your greens and browns while adding other organics such as finished compost, grass clippings from earlier, chopped up leaves, coffee grounds, kitchen scraps, seaweed, garden trimmings, sawdust and even used potting soil. Adding topsoil would speed things along so if you have it, add that to the mix as well. Make sure that your pile is at least a feet or more in depth. Top this off with a fine layer of mulch to prevent any weeds from growing. It would take several months for your materials to completely decompose.

Building a lasagna garden in the fall and planting when spring comes around would be the best way to accomplish this. By then, you'll have a lot of leaves to add to your organic matter mix. If you're building around summer or spring, you can hasten the decomposition process by adding a lot of compost and topsoil to your mix. Adding about 2 to 3 inches of topsoil and compost before you plant your seedlings always helps with the yield.

Can I use recycled wooden frames to start my raised garden?

Of course! One of the benefits of raised bed gardening/container gardening is that you can recycle old wooden frames of structures. The only limitation that you need to consider is that the wood that comprises the said frame should not have been chemically treated at any time. As stated earlier, you would want your raised flower or vegetable bed to be as natural and as chemical-free as possible.

The following are just a few of the wooden containers that you can recycle in the process of making your raised flower or vegetable garden:

1.) *Old bed frames*. Antique bed frames are generally fashioned out of rot-resistant wood (e.g., cedar or cypress) and also have a beautiful, unique look to them that would instantly enhance your raised bed garden's overall look. Should you wish to use an old bed frame to house your raised flower or vegetable garden, consider the following tips:

   a. The ideal bed frame for a raised flower or vegetable garden should have its sideboards intact. These serve to keep the soil and the plants within, preventing them from leaking out over the container. Should the antique bed frame you have in mind be lacking these, you can ask a carpenter to saw up a bit of lumber and attach the resulting side frames to the body of the bed frame. Do bear in mind that you might need to buff up the new side frames so that they match the look or the finish of the antique bed frame.

b. *As much as possible, use a child's bed frame.* While a majestic four-poster bed might strike your fancy, adult-sized bed frames have a tendency to be set rather high above the ground. This might make things awkward if you or your assigned gardeners are not particularly tall (or endowed with rather long limbs). Also, king-sized antique bed frames are a no-no. Given their widths, it would be very difficult (if not impossible) to reach the middle of the resulting raised flower or vegetable bed without considerable assistance.

2.) *Wooden fishing boats.* Should you happen to live with a fishing aficionado, you might want to consider scouring his or her workstation for wooden boats that are no longer fit for the water. Similarly, you can also try scouring some online listings for people who might be selling off their old wooden fishing boats.

Apart from adding unique aesthetic appeal to your raised flower or vegetable garden, the use of a wooden fishing boat to house a raised bed is also quite convenient. Most fishing boats are generally made to the ideal size of raised beds (i.e., with easy to reach middle portions, among other things) and are at the perfect height (not too high, not too low) for containing a raised flower or vegetable bed.

Should you find yourself hauling an old fishing boat into your garden for that very purpose, bear in mind the following tips:

a.) Watch out for any signs of rot. The last thing you want in a raised garden container is something that could fall apart with the least bit of provocation. If you are buying someone's old fishing boat, the first thing you should do is to inspect its wooden body for traces of rot.

b.) Don't forget to drill a few holes in the bottom before you line it with gardening plastic. This will help the water drain out of the raised bed easier. (This step is why you have to be absolutely sure that the boat in question has been rendered unfit for use over any body of water. It would be a shame to waste a good boat, after all.)

c.) Once the bottom of the wooden boat has been lined, you can try to even out the terrain by adding in some rocks or some newspaper. You can then fill the space with fertilized soil as well as the seeds or seedlings of your choice afterwards.

d.) To up the wooden boat's aesthetic ante, you can also paint the wooden exteriors with the color/s of your choice.

Apart from wood, what else can I use?

Metal can also work, so long as it's not misshapen or rusty. You need to keep in mind that constant contact with water tends to cause metal structures to rust over time, so recycled metal containers might be a temporary fix at best.

Still, should you be short on funds with no old wooden bed frame or fishing boat on hand, a sturdy old metal filing cabinet will do nicely for the time being. Just make sure that it's not rusting away, however.

To prepare an old filing cabinet as a base for your raised garden, the following steps are necessary:

1.) Remove all the drawers and their accompanying attachments from the filing cabinets. The drawers can be recycled for other purposes (e.g., as makeshift gardening pots or containers). Should the inside of the filing cabinet be coated in paint, it would need to be removed. Rubbing the sides with sandpaper usually does the trick.

2.) Drill a few rows of small holes into the back of the filing cabinet. (This will serve as the container's water drainage outlet.) Tip the empty filing cabinet over so that its back can serve as the base for the new flower or vegetable bed. If you don't want to drill any holes into the back of the old filing cabinet, you can also place a layer of drainage filler material at the bottom of the container. A single layer of river rock, followed by a three to four-inch layer of gravel that's topped by a three to four-inch layer of sand will suffice. (Apart from sparing you the hassle of having to power up your old drill, this alternative also helps the metal cabinet last a bit longer. The drainage filler material can soak up the water and prevent it from coming into contact with the bottom of the filing cabinet, thus holding off the rusting process.)

3.) Line the inside of the filing cabinet with your lining material of choice. Choose one with a water resistant side so as to protect the sides of the metal filing cabinet from rusting and make sure you get enough of it to cover the insides of the filing cabinet thoroughly.

4.) Repaint the outside of the filing cabinet. This is optional, of course, but it does help make the container look more attractive and cheery. Should you want to paint your recycled filing cabinet, choose water-resistant paints that are formulated to adhere to metallic surfaces in particular so that they don't chip easily.

5.) Fill the base of the filing cabinet with fertilized soil, leaving about two inches at the top.

6.) Place the flower or vegetable seeds atop the soil, carefully positioning them so that they don't overcrowd each other. Alternatively, you can also transplant flower or vegetable seedlings into the soil.

Old or new garden bricks (the ones that are made from clay or from cement) can also work. However, using them can be tricky since they come in various shapes and sizes, and you would need to layout a shape and size that can accommodate them since it would be quite difficult to cut bricks down into the sizes that you would need.

Still, once you've figured out an ideal size for your raised flower or vegetable bed and you've got your garden bricks on the ready, you can start plotting out your new garden:

1.) Choose the proper spot for your bricked-in raised garden. Ideally, it should have level ground, and there should be enough space for both the actual raised bed and the garden brick borders.

2.) Carefully level out the ground of the chosen site. You can use either a rake or a shovel to position the soil, or have your assigned gardener work on it.

3.) Assemble the brick layers to form a border around the garden plot. Begin at the bottom, laying out the garden bricks end to end. (While you can use garden bricks of varying sizes and shapes, it's much easier to use identical ones.) Make sure that they are laid next to each other quite snugly. Do the same for the next two or three layers until you get the height that you desire.

4.) Line the insides of the brick borders. You will need to use a thick sort of liner, with weed liner being the most ideal. Make sure you have enough material to cover the inside of the bricked-in box as well as its inner sides. Any excess material or liner can be trimmed off later on anyway.

5.) Fill the bricked-in box with soil and fertilizers (if needed), leaving about 2 inches at the top for some extra breathing room (though you can add a bit more soil if necessary once the seeds or seedlings have been added in).

6.) Carefully position your flower or vegetable seeds and seedlings of choice.

How can I keep the pests or insects away from my raised bed garden?

While raised bed farming or planting does a pretty good job of keeping burdensome weeds at bay, you or your gardener may still have to deal with the occasional pest or insect intruding upon your flower or vegetable plot. There's also the question of plant damage that results from exposure to the harsher elements, such as extreme wind (as well as the intrusion brought about by stray, wild, windborne seeds landing upon the raised bed).

Fortunately, you can set up your raised bed in such a way that the aforementioned disturbances can be minimized, if not entirely avoided. This is done by installing a series of hoops or arches that support a form of protective netting. It should also be noted, however, that this can only be done with raised flower or vegetable beds that have wooden frames or containers. Free form raised beds aren't exactly equipped with the kind of structure needed to support the said arches or hoops.

If you feel that your raised flower or vegetable garden might benefit from additional pest control, then you can work on the following installation:

1.) PVC pipes are the ideal material for the hoops or arches since they are quite flexible and easy to attach. Form the hoops or arches by cutting and bending the PVC pipes so that each end of the resulting hoop or arch is in contact with one side of the wooden frame or container. The advisable distance between the installed hoops or arches is about four to six feet or up to about 1.8 meters.

2.) Buy either plastic bird netting (if small birds seem especially keen on intruding upon your raised flower or vegetable garden) or spun fiber cloth (which is great for keeping insects and pests at bay) from your nearest garden supply shop. Measure out enough of your chosen material so that it will stretch across the arches and all the way over the sides of the box or frame.

3.) Clip the plastic bird netting or the spun fiber cloth (In case you can't find some of this, some gardening supply stores also refer to it as a floating row-cover.) onto the arches. Smooth out the material before clipping it onto the next arch so that it stretches tautly across the space. Make sure that the material doesn't dip down onto the flower or vegetable seedlings or touch the top of the soil bed.

The beauty of installing this pseudo-greenhouse fixture is that not only does it help protect the fruit or vegetable seedlings better, but it can also be quite economical in the long run. Keeping burdensome pests or insects at bay can reduce the need to purchase insecticides or pesticides.

However, should the flowers or vegetables in one portion of your raised bed happen to grow too tall for the protective netting, you don't have to take out the entire canopy. Simply remove the netting over the area in question, and pull it all the way down to the ground between the said area and the next. Alternatively, you can also try making a larger hoop (one that is taller than the plants in the area of concern) and replace the existing hoop at the end of the area of concern with it. You can then drape the protective netting all the way over to the new hoop.

Chapter 3: Intensive Gardening

So now that you've got your raised bed set up nicely, what else is there? Well, what use is a rich soil if you have no clue how to do proper gardening? Intensive gardening practices would only further increase the efficiency of the soil itself and make your produce even more successful.

Intensive horticulture has actually been in practice for centuries now and in many different parts of the world. In the United States, the most popular method would be the French Intensive Gardening. But of course, you can choose one depending on your preferences and whatever suits the need. Several things tie intensive gardening varieties together, and while they are each a unique discipline, there are basics that you can't replace. Among those practices would be the close spacing between the plants, the use of raised growing beds, maintaining the fertility of the soil and succession planting which allows you to make the best use of what space there is.

If applied properly and consistently, you can increase your yield by least 5 times more than what you would expect for an average garden. However, intensive gardening, as the name suggests, also requires a lot of work, scheduling and planning. More than the average row garden, as a matter of fact. This is also why a lot of people tend to avoid it or opt for something else. But, if you're really keen on the idea of growing fantastic produce then, you have to start gradually. This is especially so if you're a beginner in the field and still feeling your way around. For example, you can try building at least one or two raised garden beds every gardening soon for a couple of years until you've become more acquainted with the process.

Why the close planting space?

The reason for this is actually pretty simple, making use of all the space you have available simply gives you more yield. You'll only need to spare a few in order to give adequate spacing between crop rows and for your pathways, nothing more. If you're doing intensive gardening, make sure that you keep things tight. Plant your crops in a staggered or triangular pattern since this would allow for their leaves to overlap during maturity. Besides that, it also provides you with a kind of natural canopy created by the leaves themselves. This means that your garden bed would be well-shaded, moderating its temperature, discouraging the growth of weeds and conserves the moisture of the soil itself.

Another thing you must keep in mind when planting crops close together is having some knowledge about its growing habits. You need to plan the spaces carefully to accommodate for: root spread, nutrient and water needs as well as their size. This is why it's often recommended that you only plant one kind of crop for each garden bed. This makes it easier for you to approximate their growth pattern.

Succession Planting:

Another technique that you can use to further maximize your yield would be succession planting. This is basically the process of rapidly filling any space that's been left open by a harvested crop. Often, the replacement would be a next-season harvest. For example, you can harvest warm-season (summer) crops such as squash or beans and replace their spot with something for the cooler-season such as spinach or peas. You can also choose to stagger your planting time within 1 to 2 week intervals, doing so would prolong the harvest.

Note: Advanced intensive gardeners would also often inter-plant a variety of compatible full, mid and short season crops in the same bed, at the same time. Upon harvest, they will simply plant the faster-growing ones again. This is repeated around 2 to 4 times for every season.

Whichever intensive gardening technique you might opt for, the following tips would come in handy if you want to boost your raised garden's yield even further:

1.) *Pay close attention to the shape of your raised garden beds.* Rather than completely flattening the top of your raised garden bed, form the top of the soil into a gently-rounded arc instead. This will increase the amount of available surface area for planting significantly since resulting arc expands the base measurement (and you can also plant hardier vegetables like spinach and lettuce on the sides of the arc). For instance, a flat area that measures around five feet wide also offers only five feet worth of planting space but a rounded arc resting on a base that measures the same can yield up to twenty percent more planting space. You will thus get significantly more yield using the same amount of space.

2.) *Use certain protective devices to begin your planting period early or to extend your harvesting period.* Insulating tunnels or cold frames can make it possible for you to plant spring vegetables a month before the said season begins, and thus give you a considerable head start on the growing season. Conversely, draping your hardy autumn or winter crops with protective netting or row covers can shield them from frost (or from the perils of cold-weather animals like deer). Doing so will buy you more time to put off the harvest so that you can enjoy a more bountiful spread in the winter.

3.) *Maximize the space provided by raised beds by "going vertical."* If you built frames or borders around your raised vegetable garden, you can install trellises or fences on their sides for vine crops like tomatoes, peas, melons, squash, or cucumbers to grow on. Ideally, you should pick the sturdiest side of the raised vegetable bed for installing the climbing trellis on. Make sure you use thick, sturdy end posts so that the crops can grow and climb up without the risk of the trellis falling apart (It has been observed, however, that heavy fruits or vegetables like melons or cucumbers tend to grow thicker and stronger vines to further secure themselves onto climbing trellises.).

4.) *Be especially careful when spacing your plants.* Conventional wisdom might favor planting seeds or seedlings in straight, neat rows. However, experienced gardeners favor the triangular planting approach, where seeds or seedlings form triangular patterns together. This increases the number of seeds or seedlings that a raised vegetable bed can accommodate by as much as ten percent, and also keeps weeds or pests at bay since the space between the seeds or seedlings is considerably tightened. However, you should also make it a point to allot enough breathing room between the seeds or seedlings. Placing them too close together can result in overcrowding, particularly when they start to bud and blossom. This can prevent some plant species from achieving their full size and can even result in them being more vulnerable to certain diseases or insects.

5.) *Interplant compatible crops.* This not only saves space but increases the yield capacity of a raised flower or vegetable bed considerably too. For a list of compatible crop combinations, you can refer to the seventh chapter of this book.

6.) *Cultivate crops that have a naturally high yield.* No matter how well you plan your garden, space out your seedlings or shape your raised vegetable bed, it will all be for nothing if you chose to plant a vegetable crop that naturally produces very little yield to begin with. Apart from hardy winter fruits like squash, lettuce, or peas, you can also try chatting up your local gardeners or produce farmers to find out which sorts of crops grow well (i.e., yield a considerable quantity) your area. Bear in mind that in some cases, you might have to cultivate hybrid varieties which are better equipped than their purebred counterparts at warding off insect infestations and diseases to truly get the high yield benefits of certain vegetables like sweet bell peppers.

7.) *Choose fast-maturing crops.* This is particularly crucial if you choose to implement succession planning since vegetable crops that mature fast give you a head start in prepping the soil for the next batch of crops (thus increasing your expected yield considerably). Examples of these include fast-maturing corn or winter garlic.

8.) *Whenever possible, use transplants or seedlings.* Using transplants or seedlings of fast-maturing vegetable crops as opposed to using seeds eliminates the considerable wait that the germination process would entail. Direct-seeded plants (those that are grown by putting seeds into the soil) can take up to a month longer than their transplant or seedling counterparts to grow and mature. Furthermore, transplants or seedlings are also hardier than seeds. Thus, the likelihood of all the transplants or seedlings turning into full-grown vegetables becomes much higher, increasing the overall yield of the chosen crop.

9.) *Include kitchen herbs like basil or tarragon.* These can usually be planted in the corners of the raised vegetable beds. Cultivating essential kitchen herbs not only increases both your yield and your garden's variety, but it can also save you a great deal of money. Growing your own herbs cost about a fraction of their retail price at the average supermarket, and as an added bonus, you'll always have fresh herbs on hand.

10.) *Try planting a new vegetable crop every season.* While an abundance of tomatoes is a great idea in theory, no one is really keen on having to eat them all year. When one phase of your succession planning scheme ends, that is usually the perfect time to introduce a new vegetable specimen into the mix. If you really want to go the extra mile, you can start cultivating the said vegetable specimen's seeds in pots about a month before planting them so that you can use the resulting transplants. For those who want a variety of vegetable crops on the ready, you can also assign a specific raised vegetable bed for the sole purpose of growing the said variety. Bok choy lettuce, fennel, radicchio, and white beets are just some of the more unusual but delicious vegetable varieties that you can attempt to cultivate.

11.) *Grow vegetables or crops that automatically regenerate after every harvest.* Certain vegetables are equipped with stalks and leaves that grow back when cut or harvested. Some vegetables, like broccoli or bulb fennel, can regrow their green leafy heads after two or three harvests (provided that you snip them above a certain height). Not only will these kinds of crops increase your yield significantly, but they can also make things more convenient for you by eliminating the need to germinate seeds and replant the resulting transplants after every harvest.

12.) *If you have limited space, choose perennials over their seasonal counterparts.* Not only do perennial plants require significantly less maintenance than their seasonal counterparts (i.e., no need to replant), but their resilient and hardy natures also ensure a steady and bountiful harvest every year.

13.) *Replant vegetable roots.* Bulb vegetables are ideal for this purpose, though you can also use the root cuttings of other vegetables to regrow the crop. This practice can increase your yield considerably since plants that are regrown from roots or root cuttings grow and mature at nearly the same rate as transplants do. Replanting vegetable roots will also stretch a vegetable crop's shelf life. For instance, you can take the cuttings of a certain vegetable in the summer and then replant these shortly before autumn. Thus, you end up with two harvests of the same crop within the year as opposed to just one.

14.) *Harvest crops early and often.* Doing so prolongs a crop's reproduction cycle, thus increasing the total annual yield considerably. (However, if you still want to enjoy a crop's full flavor and freshness despite harvesting it early, opt to pick them early in the morning. Plants are usually at their best before 10 am, when they are all plumped up with water and nutrients from the earth.) Bear in mind, however, that you might need to allocate space in your refrigerator or chiller for certain vegetables like leafy greens and cucumbers if you opt to harvest early and often.

15.)   *Don't forget to water your crops often.* Given that raised vegetable beds were designed to drain water efficiently, you can expect that you'll need to water them more often to ensure that they grow and mature properly (and thus provide you with a higher yield). If you're wary about rising water costs, however, you can also consider bringing in water-efficient aids like mulches or soaker hoses.

Chapter 4: Great Garden Vegetables for Beginners

Arugula

- Easy to grow and harvesting it is very quick to do. This would add a nutty and aromatic note to your salads. Arugula can be planted in simple window boxes or containers if you don't have much space. They grow even better when grown in a raised garden bed, however. You can get these in either seed or starter plant form.

Cherry Belle Radish

- These are easy to grow and can be stored to ripen later. If this is your first time planting radishes, these would be a great variety to start with. Maintenance is simple and you get results quickly.

Black Seed Simpson Lettuce

- There are 2 different types of lettuce: the heading varieties such as romaine, iceberg and Boston The other type would be the loose leaf varieties which is perfect for raised bed gardening, especially if you're trying out succession planting. These grow quickly and are easy to plant. For beginners, these would be a great crop to try out.

Spinach

- Quite unlike other vegetables, spinach would grow in a shaded area (or at least one that gets direct sunlight for 4 to 6 hours a day) as well as in full sun. This means, it's one of the easier plants to find a spot for her. Just make sure the area isn't too shady or else it won't grow at all.

Contender Bush Beans

- There are plenty of uses for these. The beans can be eaten fresh or dried for long term use. The heirloom variety is the most flavorful. They are also pretty easy to grow and cultivate so if you're looking for a bean crop, do consider this.

Sugar Ann Snap Peas

- Best for spring gardens and is also quite easy to plant though it takes a little longer than most to grow. You just need to make sure that the vines don't get smothered and that they have ample space to spread. Building firmly grounded trellises are a must.

Beets

- This one is easy to plan and even easier to grow for as long as your soil can be worked with in spring. For raised garden beds, they are more among the most appropriate crops for they don't need a lot of space and can be planted in close proximity with other plants.

Carrots

- A perennial favorite. This can be planted as soon as your soil is ready. Make sure it is well fertilized, however. They thrive the best in fertile sandy loam but that isn't necessary for you to be able to yield a good amount of this crop.

Cucumbers

- Always give your cucumber plants generous amounts of different organic matter and make sure that the soil remains well-fertilized. Doing this regularly would yield crunchy cucumbers and also efficiently increase your harvest.

Basil

- Plant your basil seeds in moist, rich soil in an area that receives direct sunlight. For continual harvest, make sure that you sow your basil every few weeks.

Dill

- This herb is great because you can use it in its fresh or dry form. However, to make sure that your seeds thrive, plant them in warmer areas of your garden bed. The best temperature for these would be around 75 to 80 degrees Fahrenheit.

Tomatoes

- You'll have to plant these in areas where they'll get a lot of sun. The smaller varieties such as cherry tomatoes are recommended for beginners. You will also need to provide some type of support such as a stake or a cage to make sure they grow well. It has been said that the less you water them, the tastier they become. However, don't completely neglect them.

Zucchini

- Much like beans and cucumbers, these plants are also prolific regardless of where you plant them. However, they grow better in mounded soul and would need good moisture as well as warmth. So choose a place that constantly has sunlight upon it during the day. Planting it is best done during warmer seasons too, making it one of the best choices for when you're procrastinating on your gardening.

Mint

- One of the most popular herbs, the delicate, leafy mint can grow virtually anywhere so long as it is watered regularly. For best results, you can try planting mint alongside other crops like carrots or potatoes so that it doesn't overtake the raised bed. (Mint leaves have a tendency to grow quickly and widely if left unchecked.) Apart from being used as a garnish, mint leaves can also be chewed after a meal as an all-natural breath freshener.

Garlic

- Not only are garlic bulbs easy to grow, but they also attract beneficial wasps that prey on other pests. And growing them could not be easier. All you need to do is plant a few cloves of garlic into your raised bed (the efficient drainage feature of the raised vegetable bed is particularly beneficial for garlic since it thrives on well-drained soil), and water it a few times. They're best planted in the spring or in early autumn so that you can enjoy a fuss-free harvest in the summer.

Onions

- Onion bulbs can be cultivated alongside garlic, as they both require virtually zero maintenance and can pretty much take care of themselves. Like garlic bulbs, onion bulbs are best planted either in the spring or in the early autumn so that they can be harvested in the summer. One of the best things about onions is that you only need to cultivate their transplants once: you can simply cut off the bases of the onion bulbs for planting each time you harvest a new crop.

Pole beans

- Since they are vertically grown (i.e., on a trellis), pole beans take up very little space. They also don't require much effort to maintain, but planting them alongside plants that have lengthy stalks can speed up their vining process. Apart from having a considerably high yield (especially when they are harvested frequently), pole beans also attract good bugs that serve to keep noxious pests away from the other plants.

Runner beans

- Runner beans are also climbers that can save you a great deal of space. Though you might need to set up a fair bit of space for them at the beginning, they are quite easy to maintain. Regular watering sessions and frequent harvesting are usually enough to help them flourish. And if you don't have the luxury of space, you can also try cultivating the dwarfish runner bean varieties instead.

Spring onions

- Crunchy and peppery, the green-white spring onion stalks can be transplanted from pots after their seeds have germinated, or they can be sown directly onto the soil of your raised vegetable bed. They too require only a fair bit of watering and are best planted throughout the summer months.

Bell peppers

- There are lots of bell pepper varieties to choose from, and most of them are quite easy to plant if you begin with a starter plant. Gardening stores and plant nurseries are usually well-stocked with a good variety of bell pepper starter plants, so you can just visit one and take your pick.

Potatoes

- This starchy root crop is a staple in many cultures, and it's no real wonder considering how easy it is to grow once the ground has been prepped properly. Best grown about a couple of months before the spring season, potatoes need to be planted in fertile soil with a lot of compost. Once green shoots begin to sprout from the ground, simply cover the lot with more compost and then keep watering them for about 10-20 weeks (depending on the variety you planted). Once the green shoots turn yellow and start to wither, you can already begin harvesting.

Cilantro

- Cilantro is a pungent staple in Mexican cuisine and is usually grown by sowing coriander seeds into the soil. It grows pretty fast, especially when watered frequently, so it needs to be harvested throughout the season as well. But given that it's a mainstay of the traditional salsa, you should have no trouble making use of this herb's bountiful harvest.

Oregano

- If you're a big fan of Italian food, you can try growing your own oregano. This leafy, aromatic herb is a hardy perennial that thrives throughout the year despite very little maintenance and is a great asset to any food lover's garden. And since it needs to be harvested throughout the year as well, you'll never be at a loss for fresh oregano should you feel the need to whip up your own pasta or pizza sauce.

Swiss chard

- These vibrant, multi-colored greens can be planted alternately with spinach throughout the year. Like its beet cousins, it thrives in raised vegetable beds and container gardens and is rather easy to cultivate and maintain.

These are just some of the easier, common garden vegetables that any beginner could try their hand with. Once you've got the hang of raised bed gardening, you can expand your selection and try ones that might need a bit more work to grow properly and successfully. But to get there, you need to practice a bit and familiarize yourself with the different processes involved.

Chapter 5: Easy to Grow Flowers for Beginners

Sweet peas

- The great thing about these is that the more you pick, the more flowers they'll produce unlike other plants. They have large seeds that are pretty easy to handle but if sowing isn't your forte then you can also choose to go with sweet pea plug plants. All these plants really need is a sunny area to grow in, plenty of water and a support fence. Slugs and snails can become a problem but with constant care, this shouldn't be too big of an issue.

Nigella

- Looking for something easy that doesn't require much maintenance? These are the flowers for you. All you really need to do is scatter the seeds over your raised garden bed and it pretty much looks after itself. A little watering, some sun and it will produce bright blue flowers. The plant is much tougher than it looks, however, and when the flowers fade it sets the seed by itself which would grow the following year.

Aquilegia

- These are easy to grow flowering plants which would come back year after year once you've begun planting them. You can start things off in a small pot, then transplant them to the garden bend once they've sprouted enough. These plants can tolerate any kind of environment conditions and would thrive in the sun or in semi-shade.

Californian Poppy

- If you're not too fond of plants that constantly need watering then this would make for a good option to try. These colorful annuals thrive better in dry, poor soil that is in direct sunlight thus making them great for the areas of your garden that doesn't have the best soil quality. Scatter them all over the area and they basically take care of themselves. However, a little watering every now and then never hurt just make sure that you don't get over zealous with it.

Nasturtium

- Now this is one flowering plant that even kids can grow. Sow them along the sides of your raised garden bed, directly onto the soil. The best bit about them is they don't need much tending to. As long as your soil is healthy, they would grow quite abundantly as well. These are edible as well so they're a feast for both your eyes and palate.

Marigold

- These bedding plants, much like the nasturtium are also very easy to grow, especially for beginners. The seeds are easy enough to handle and if you opt for the taller variety, you'll only need to put a few stakes or fencing in to support it. Any area that gets ample sun would be good for this plant.

Geranium (Cranesbill)

- Another low maintenance and sturdy flowering plant, this also makes for a great ground cover and would bloom into small purple flowers year after year. You can grow them from seeds and bare roots depending on what's easier for you. Choose an area of your garden bed that gets just enough sun for these, and they will basically take care of themselves.

Fuchsias

- These are typically, best grown from plugs as seeds can be a little tricky. However, they do make great practice for the beginner gardener so if you're up for a challenge, you can try both. The climbing variety, Lady Boothby, would need a little bit of extra care and some support but otherwise, these are still relatively easy to grow. Trimming it every now and then would also encourage more growth.

Pansies

- These ones are easy to grow from seeds and can be planted regardless of the season. They don't need much maintenance other than making sure to deadhead the wilted flowers to encourage more abundant growth. Plant them in areas that get enough sunlight. They grow abundantly and quite quickly so beginners would certainly have a lot of fun tending to these plants.

Poppies

- These require very little as well and are easy to grow from seed. Sow them into the garden bed directly during the cooler (or even rainy) weather in order to help germinate the seeds. Maintenance isn't a very big thing for this as well, just make sure it gets enough sunlight and water. Well fertilized soil would do wonders for its growth and the vibrancy of its blooms.

Cosmos

- Planning on an annual garden? This would be one of the best plants to add to your selection. It's very low maintenance and even thrives in areas where the soil isn't so great. A little sun, water and a bit of fertilizer would certain go a long way when it comes to it. Expect foliage-like daisy shaped flowers in varying shades of yellow, pink, orange and magenta to cover your garden once it blooms.

Sunflowers

- Sunflower seeds can be sown directly onto your raised flower bed once spring starts to give way to summer. They're fairly low-maintenance, but you should steer clear of planting sunflower transplants onto your raised flower bed since sunflower cuttings fare better when grown in their own pots. And if you're worried about the space that sunflowers can take up, you can compensate by planting beans at the base of the sprouting sunflowers since the former can sprout stalks that will support the latter.

Zinnia

- One of the hardier summer flowers, zinnia seeds don't take long to germinate once they are planted into fertile ground during the warm summer months. Provided that they are watered frequently, zinnia seeds will bloom into vibrant and fragrant blooms before too long.

Russian sage

- These delicate blue flowers are generally better-suited to larger gardens since they can grow as tall as five feet. However, the Russian sage is also a hardy perennial that is resistant to the occasional summer drought. (It is actually known to thrive on constant exposure to the sun.) If you want to try growing these, you can relegate them to the back of the raised flower bed so that they'll have enough room to grow.

Perennial sage

- As a relation of the famed kitchen herb, the perennial sage is also a perennial that is particularly adept at withstanding freezing weather. However, this variety is also a big fan of sunlight (much like its cousins in the sage family), so you should plant in on a spot of the raised flower bed where it will get adequate exposure to the sun.

Purple coneflower

- These tall, typically purple wildflowers thrive during the summer and don't require much watering as they have a high tolerance for heat and drought. Since these prairie-born wildflowers adore the sun, you should also plant them in spots on the raised flower bed that get a great deal of sunlight.

Veronica

- These tall, spiky flowers come in varieties that can grow and thrive everywhere from the cold North to the sunny South. Thus, depending on the variety you choose, you can have colorful Veronica flowers dotting your flower bed from early summer all the way through to the start of autumn.

Asters

- Though they are partial to the fall season, aster blooms can also prosper in the late summer, when the temperatures start to drop. Aster flowers come in a wide range of colors, from bright white to ruby red, and look particularly striking when they're planted along a raised flower bed's borders.

Yarrow

- This medicinal flower is so resistant to all sorts of extreme weather (e.g., hot droughts and freezing winds) that it grows practically everywhere without much effort. Yarrow plants can also exhibit an impressive array of colors that change along with the seasons. Bright pinks, yellows, and reds are the norm for those flower clusters that bloom in late spring, while gray green ferns that emit an earthy, spicy scent abound in early autumn.

Daffodils

- Daffodil bulbs are unfailing perennials that blossom throughout the year, particularly during the various stages of the spring season. Daffodil seeds can be allowed to germinate in separate pots, and then transplanted onto raised flower beds, but after that, they only require regular watering. Generally, the daffodil plant's narrow leaves make an appearance shortly before the fragrant, multi-colored flowers finally emerge.

Black-eyed Susan

- These typically yellow blooms with their bold black centers (hence the whimsical name) bloom throughout the lengthy period between the middle of the summer months and the onset of the winter frost. Like most perennials, black-eyed Susan flowers are resistant to heat and drought, and are best planted in the middle or the back of the raised flower bed (where they will have enough room to grow as well as adequate sunlight).

Hardy hibiscus

- Characterized by their vibrant, contrasting colors and their humongous size (some varieties can grow as big as dinner plates), the hardy hibiscus may take time to sprout since it only begins to germinate once the temperatures start to rise and the soil begins to heat up. Once the sun starts warming up your garden once again, however, you can practically leave the Hardy Hibiscus alone to grow and flourish in the rich and regularly watered soil of your raised flower bed.

Chrysanthemum

- Prized by the Chinese and Japanese as the floral symbol of friendship, these multi-petal blooms can resemble fireworks once they bloom in your autumn garden. Though they're quite easy to cultivate and take care of, you might want to consider replanting them every few years or so since they can sometimes die out after a few seasons.

So there you have it, a short list of easy to grow flowers that require very little maintenance in order for them to grow. These are great for beginners who are still trying to find their way around tending and growing flowering plants. Consider it your training towards the trickier plant varieties.

Chapter 6: Raised Bed Gardening Tips

- Make sure that you plan your raised garden bed exactly how you want it from the very start because changing and moving it can be very difficult later on. A tip is to make it adaptable so that you'll be able to add more raised beds should it be needed.

- Make sure that there is ample space between each bed for you to move around in. You may think that connecting 1 or 2 together would make it easier but this can only end up limiting the working space available. So keep them nicely spaced so you can walk around each bed and do what needs to be done. Keep in mind that you might need to use bigger tools such as hoes and wheelbarrows so do prepare for these as well.

- Set up your irrigation system. Drip lines are pretty cheap and easy to install but another option you can try are soaker hoses. Whichever one you choose, remember to place the water line under your mulch as this would prevent evaporation. A sprinkler only wastes water and leaves moisture on the leaves which can lead to various fungal diseases.

- Position your garden beds so that they get the most amount of sunlight possible. Keep in mind that many vegetables prefer direct sun and would thrive better in areas that are open and get plenty of exposure. Make sure that your raised beds get at least 8 hours of sunlight a day but going above that is even better. If you're planting vegetables that require less, make use of a shade cover or plant taller vegetables around it which should help create a natural shade.

- Always plan your crops ahead of time. Doing this would allow you to better determine just how much space you're going to need. Creating a layout of your vegetable and flower beds is also a great idea to help you better visualize the space you'll be working with. Check the seed packets for information as well as space recommendations. This is important to avoid the spread of infection and fungal diseases.

- Organizing compost. It would be best if you kept your compost bin near the garden itself. Your vegetables would eventually produce waste material which you'll have to deal with and composting is basically recycling those. Remember that using compost, which contains a lot of organic matter, in your garden beds would contribute to a more abundant yield for it provides your plants with all the nutrients that it needs to thrive. Not to mention the fact that it actually holds water really well thus effectively reducing your irrigation needs. You'll be able to save a lot of money this way as well. Always make sure that you have a good supply of this for your garden and that it is readily and conveniently available.

- Consider companion planting as a means of maximizing the space that you have. There are numerous plants that actually serve other purposes such as repelling pests while there are those that help enrich the soil through their nitrogen fixing properties. The legume family helps a lot with the latter and are also great crops for raised garden beds. You may also consider planting herbs along with your vegetables along with some flowers. While it may not protect your garden completely, it will certainly help when it comes to minimizing crop loss which is often due to insect infestation.

These are just a few of the tips that every beginner gardener (as well as more experienced ones) must remember when it comes to properly tending their raised bed gardens. These would help improve your yield as well as the condition of the soil as well.

Chapter 7: Companion Planting Combinations

Diversity is one of the key things that every good gardener tries to achieve in cultivating a garden. While the sight of various plants in every size, shape, and color may delight the eye, there is actually a far more functional angle to planting different crops side by side. The concept of companion planning, which was introduced in the previous chapter, hinges on the fact that certain plants can help each other's growth and maturation processes immensely.

Apart from maximizing the space efficiency of raised flower or vegetable beds, companion planting also offers the following benefits:

1.) Some plants attract good bugs and insects into the garden or into the raised bed, which could benefit one or two of the plants growing within the same space. The said insects, which usually prey on noxious pests, are thus compelled to stay on. This inadvertently allows the other plants to grow and mature largely without any disturbance from the said pests. Conversely, there are also some plant species that lure bad bugs and pests away from their more vulnerable counterparts.

2.) Tall plants, when cultivated alongside ones that are photosensitive, can serve as natural umbrellas that protect the latter and prevent them from dying due to too much sun exposure. Plants that grow by creeping up on trellises or frames can also provide shade for their neighbors, provided that their trellises or frames are facing the sun.

3.) There are also some plants that serve to repel or ward off pests and insects. Cucumbers, for instance, are known to repel ants as the insects can't seem to stand the natural aroma that they give off. Planting them alongside sweet fruits like strawberries can thus prevent the onslaught of ants.

Should you want to try out companion planning, any of the following suggested combinations would serve you well:

1.) *Beans, squash, and corn.* Long cherished by the Native Americans as the "three sisters" of root crops, this triumvirate works because the structure and growth process of each plant somehow benefits the others. The squash plant, which usually grows close to the ground, keeps the weeds at bay. The corn plant, on the other hand, sprouts stalks that serve as a natural trellis for the bean's vines. The beans, for their part, attract insects like fall armyworms, leaf beetles, and leafhoppers, all of whom prey on the pests that like to prey on corn stalks.

2.) *Cucumbers and nasturtiums.* Like the cucumber, the nasturtium grows on a vine, so they can easily be cultivated side by side. In addition to this, nasturtium is also known to keep pests that are harmful to the cucumber plant at bay. Apart from serving as a natural habitat for spiders and ground beetles (which are said to prey on insects that target cucumbers), nasturtiums are also known to repel cucumber beetles that tend to eat away at the tubular green plant's flesh and leaves.

3.) *Roses and garlic.* When planted side by side, the white garlic bulbs and the red or white rose buds may look like an odd combination. However, gardeners have been planting them side by side for centuries since rose pests are said to be put off by the odor given off by garlic cloves.

4.) *Carrots and onions.* As a member of the Allium family, onions can repel rabbits and carrot flies, which are all counted as the carrot's natural predators.

5.) *Tomatoes and cabbages.* Cabbage leaves are often victimized by caterpillars that feed on them. Tomatoes, however, are renowned for repelling caterpillars and other such larva from so much as setting foot near the cabbages when the two crops are planted side by side.

6.) *Eggplants and marigolds.* Another odd vegetable and flower combination, marigold flowers are traditionally planted alongside eggplants since the former are adept at controlling the nematodes from getting out of hand in the roots of the latter. (For this same reason, melon plants, which also have nematodes in their roots, are often planted in the same plot as marigold flowers.)

7.) *Radishes and spinach.* Planting the white bulbs alongside the green spinach sprouts protects the latter from leaf miner infestations. Since leaf miners enjoy munching their way through spinach leaves (hence their name), the lush green leaves sprouted by growing radish bulbs can attract them away from their usual prey. And since the radish bulbs can continue to grow undisturbed despite the occasional leaf miner burrowing through their leaves, the combination makes for an ideal arrangement.

8.) *Cleome, necotiana, and lettuce.* Also called the spider flower and the flowering tobacco, respectively, cleome and necotiana plants grow to a considerable height. When planted alongside the rather photosensitive lettuce plant, the flowery duo can thus provide an adequate amount of shade for the leafy vegetable to grow in. It should also be noted that one or the other will still serve the same function should there only be room for one of them.

9.) *Collards and catnip.* Flea-beetles are the ultimate enemies of the green, leafy collard plant. Experienced gardeners thus plant catnip in the same beds as collard greens since the former can excrete a substance that repels the said pests.

10.) *Cabbages and dill.* The feathery dill herb has a limp, droopy texture, so it needs to be supported by solid, hardy vegetables like cabbages. In return, the dill herb attracts wasps that keep cabbage pests like cabbage worms and beetles at bay.

11.) *Potatoes and sweet alyssum.* Apart from imbuing a sweet fragrance wherever it is planted, alyssum flowers also attract good bugs that prey on pests with a taste for starchy root crops like potatoes.

12.) *Broccoli and sweet alyssum.* The arching broccoli plants can also benefit from the tiny, predatory wasps that sweet alyssum flowers attract. The latter's blossoms also make for a stunning contrast when allowed to grow and flourish underneath the green broccoli florets.

13.) *Dwarf zinnias and cauliflowers.* The dwarf zinnia flowers release a kind of nectar that is particularly attractive to ladybugs, which in turn, keep the insects that prey on the cauliflower away.

14.) *Celery, onions, broccoli.* When planted alongside the broccoli crops, the natural sharpness of celery and onions helps to enhance their neighboring vegetable's flavor and taste.

Conclusion

One of the best things about gardening is that you can achieve the best results with relatively little effort and preparation. There's virtually no limit to what you can do with a few seeds, water, sunlight, and a bit of rich, moist earth (as well as some tender loving care). Raised bed gardening is a prime example of this. Its features and advantages allow for a wide range of possibilities, and you need only a fair bit of elbow grease and planning to transform a tiny bit of land into an abundant cornucopia of choice flowers and/or vegetables.

You should likewise bear in mind that raised bed gardening also entails a certain amount of commitment. If you truly want to have an abundance of flowers and/or vegetables in your backyard (and at your fingertips), you should also be prepared to put in the effort required to ensure a bountiful harvest. This is especially necessary if you also decide to carry out succession planting, which involves maintaining a set of raised flower or vegetable beds on a permanent basis.

However, as with anything worth pursuing, the rewards of establishing and maintaining your own raised flower or vegetable beds will far outweigh the initial cost and effort required.

Thank you again for purchasing this book!

I hope this book was able to help you to better understand what raised garden beds are and how you can get started with using them to grow different crops such as vegetables and flowers.

The next step is to take what you have learned and start with your project. This guide is meant to walk you through the process itself, to help make sure that you start off of the right foot as you familiarize yourself with this type of gardening. Just keep all of the tips in mind and do a little extra research on the side. We can guarantee that you'll be able to start growing your own produce in no time at all!

Finally, if you enjoyed this book, please take the time to share your thoughts and post a review on Amazon. We do our best to reach out to readers and provide the best value we can. Your positive review will help us achieve that. It'd be greatly appreciated!

Thank you and good luck!

Check Out My Other Books

Below you'll find some of my other popular books that are popular on Amazon and Kindle as well. Simply click on the links below to check them out. Alternatively, you can visit my author page on Amazon to see other work done by me.

Coconut Oil for Skin Care & Hair Loss

http://amzn.to/1p0GwGC

Coconut Oil & Weight Loss for Beginners

http://amzn.to/1jqdy3R

Walk Your Way To Weight Loss

http://amzn.to/1jOHpgy

Quick Easy Healthy Snack Ideas for Kids

http://amzn.to/1grvURn

Oil Pulling for Beginners

http://amzn.to/SBDoXb

Healing Babies & Children With Aromatherapy For Beginners

The Ultimate Guide to Raised Bed Gardening for Beginners

http://amzn.to/TOHJHs

Carb Cycling for Fast Easy Weight Loss

http://amzn.to/THn8Vl

Beauty Products for Beginners

http://amzn.to/1nVvwNw

Body Lotions for Beginners

http://amzn.to/S3XlWh

Container Gardening for Beginners

http://amzn.to/1oLb2po

Vegetable Gardening for beginners

http://amzn.to/1lqCCIK

Raised Bed Gardening for beginners

http://amzn.to/1nHY0ry

Greenhouse Gardening for beginners

http://amzn.to/UEmOr2

Companion Gardening for beginners

http://amzn.to/1hYzeEl

Essential Oils Box Set #1 Healing Babies and Children With Aromatherapy for Beginners & Oil Pulling for Beginners

http://amzn.to/1yZoHoQ

Essential Oils Box Set #2 Carb Cycling For Fast Easy Weight Loss + Walk Your Way to Weight Loss

http://amzn.to/Tu5xiL

Essential Oils Box Set #3 Beauty Products For Beginners + Body Lotions For Beginners

http://amzn.to/1qnVLNQ

Essential Oils Box Set #4 Coconut Oil & Weigh Loss for Beginners & Coconut Oil for Skin Care & Hair Loss

http://amzn.to/1iQQUlN

Essential Oils Box Set #5 Coconut Oil Skin Care & Hair Loss + Healing Babies & Children & Aromatherapy for Beginners + Beauty Products for Beginners +Body Lotions For Beginners +Oil Pulling for Beginners

http://amzn.to/1qGPc6D

Essential Oils Box Set #6Carb Cycling for Fast Easy Weight Loss + Oil Pulling Therapy For Beginners + Walk Your Way to Weight Loss + Coconut Oil & Weight for Beginners + Coconut Oil for Skin Care & Hair Loss

http://amzn.to/UXAAoz

Essential Oils Box Set #7 Coconut Oil for Skin Care & Hair Loss + Oil Pulling Therapy For Beginners + Healing Babies and Children with Aromatherapy for Beginners

http://amzn.to/1nUdbg5

Gardening Box Set #1 Raised Bed Gardening For Beginners + Vegetable Gardening For Beginners + Companion Gardening For Beginners + Greenhouse Gardening for Beginners +Container Gardening for Beginners

http://amzn.to/1lZOsse

Gardening Box Set #2 Container Gardening For Beginners + Ultimate Guide to Companion Gardening for Beginners

http://amzn.to/1q4wma5

If the links do not work, for whatever reason, you can simply search for these titles on the Amazon website to find them.

.

Lightning Source UK Ltd.
Milton Keynes UK
UKOW04n1646010218
317211UK00002B/30/P